Poems of Cheer by Ella

Poetry is a fascinating use of language. With almost a million words at its command it is not surprising that these Isles have produced some of the most beautiful, moving and descriptive verse through the centuries. In this series we look at the world through the eyes and minds of our most gifted poets to bring you a unique poetic guide to their lives.

Born on November 5th 1850 in Johnstown, Wisconsin, Ella Wheeler was the youngest of four children. She began to write as a child and by the time she graduated was already well known as a poet throughout Wisconsin.

Regarded more as a popular poet than a literary poet her most famous work 'Solitude' reflects on a train journey she made where giving comfort to a distressed fellow traveller she wrote how the others grief imposed itself for a time on her 'Laugh and the world laughs with you, Weep and you weep alone'. It was published in 1883 and was immensely popular.

The following year, 1884, she married Robert Wilcox. They lived for a time in New York before moving to Connecticut. Their only child, a son, died shortly after birth. It was around this time they developed an interest in spiritualism which for Ella would develop further into an interest in the occult. In later years this and works on positive thinking would occupy much of her writing.

On Robert's death in 1916 she spent months waiting for word from him from 'the other side' which never came.

In 1918 she published her autobiography The Worlds And I.

Ella died of cancer on October 30th, 1919.

Index Of Poems

The Ocean of Song
"It might have been"
Momus, God of Laughter
I Dream
The Sonnet
The Past
A Dream
Uselessness
Will
Winter Rain
Life
Burdened
Let them go
Five Kisses
Retrospection
Helena
Nothing Remains
Comrades
What Gain?
To the West
The Land of Content
Warning
After the Battles are over
And they are dumb
Night
All for me
Into Space
Through Dim Eyes
The Punished
Half Fledged
The Year
The Unattained
In the crowd
Life and I
Guerdon
Snowed Under
"Leudemanns-on-the-river"
Little Blue Hood
No Spring
Midsummer
A Reminiscence
A Girl's Faith
Two
Slipping Away
Is it done?
A Leaf
Aesthetic

WORTH WHILE
It is easy enough to be pleasant
When life flows by like a song,
But the man worthwhile is the one who will smile
When everything goes dead wrong.
For the test of the heart is trouble,
And it always comes with the years,
And the smile that is worth the praises of earth
Is the smile that shines through tears.

It is easy enough to be prudent
When nothing tempts you to stray,
When without or within no voice of sin
Is luring your soul away;
But it's only a negative virtue
Until it is tried by fire,
And the life that is worth the honour on earth
Is the one that resists desire.

By the cynic, the sad, the fallen,
Who had no strength for the strife,
The world's highway is cumbered to-day

They make up the sum of life;
But the virtue that conquers passion,
And the sorrow that hides in a smile
It is these that are worth the homage on earth,
For we find them but once in a while.

THE HOUSE OF LIFE

All wondering, and eager-eyed, within her portico
I made my plea to Hostess Life, one morning long ago.

"Pray show me this great house of thine, nor close a single door;
But let me wander where I will, and climb from floor to floor!

For many rooms, and curious things, and treasures great and small
Within your spacious mansion lie, and I would see them all."

Then Hostess Life turned silently, her searching gaze on me,
And with no word, she reached her hand, and offered up the key.

It opened first the door of Hope, and long I lingered there,
Until I spied the room of Dreams, just higher by a stair.

And then a door whereon the one word "Happiness" was writ;
But when I tried the little key I could not make it fit.

It turned the lock of Pleasure's room, where first all seemed so bright -
But after I had stayed awhile it somehow lost its light.

And wandering down a lonely hall, I came upon a room
Marked "Duty," and I entered it, to lose myself in gloom.

Along the shadowy halls I groped my weary way about,
And found that from dull Duty's room, a door of Toil led out.

It led out to another door, whereon a crimson stain
Made sullenly against the dark these words: "The Room of Pain."

But oh the light, the light, the light, that spilled down from above
And upward wound, the stairs of Faith, right to the Tower of Love!

And when I came forth from that place, I tried the little key -
And lo! the door of Happiness swung open, wide and free.

A SONG OF LIFE

In the rapture of life and of living,
I lift up my heart and rejoice,
And I thank the great Giver for giving
The soul of my gladness a voice.
In the glow of the glorious weather,
In the sweet-scented, sensuous air,
My burdens seem light as a feather
They are nothing to bear.

In the strength and the glory of power,
In the pride and the pleasure of wealth
(For who dares dispute me my dower
Of talents and youth-time and health?),
I can laugh at the world and its sages
I am greater than seers who are sad,
For he is most wise in all ages
Who knows how to be glad.

I lift up my eyes to Apollo,
The god of the beautiful days,
And my spirit soars off like a swallow,
And is lost in the light of its rays.
Are you troubled and sad? I beseech you
Come out of the shadows of strife
Come out in the sun while I teach you
The secret of life.

Come out of the world, come above it
Up over its crosses and graves,
Though the green earth is fair and I love it,
We must love it as masters, not slaves.
Come up where the dust never rises
But only the perfume of flowers
And your life shall be glad with surprises
Of beautiful hours.
Come up where the rare golden wine is
Apollo distills in my sight,
And your life shall be happy as mine is,
And as full of delight.

PRAYER
I do not undertake to say
That literal answers come from Heaven,
But I know this, that when I pray
A comfort, a support is given
That helps me rise o'er earthly things

As larks soar up on airy wings.

In vain the wise philosopher
Points out to me my fabric's flaws,
In vain the scientists aver
That "all things are controlled by laws."
My life has taught me day by day
That it availeth much to pray.

I do not stop to reason out
The why and how. I do not care,
Since I know this, that when I doubt,
Life seems a blackness of despair,
The world a tomb; and when I trust,
Sweet blossoms spring up in the dust.

Since I know in the darkest hour,
If I lift up my soul in prayer,
Some sympathetic, loving Power
Sends hope and comfort to me there.
Since balm is sent to ease my pain,
What need to argue or explain?

Prayer has a sweet, refining grace,
It educates the soul and heart.
It lends a lustre to the face,
And by its elevating art
It gives the mind an inner sight
That brings it near the Infinite.

From our gross selves it helps us rise
To something which we yet may be.
And so I ask not to be wise,
If thus my faith is lost to me.
Faith, that with angel's voice and touch
Says, "Pray, for prayer availeth much."

IN THE LONG RUN

In the long run fame finds the deserving man.
The lucky wight may prosper for a day,
But in good time true merit leads the van
And vain pretence, unnoticed, goes its way.
There is no Chance, no Destiny, no Fate,
But Fortune smiles on those who work and wait,
In the long run.

In the long run all godly sorrow pays,
There is no better thing than righteous pain,
The sleepless nights, the awful thorn-crowned days,
Bring sure reward to tortured soul and brain.
Unmeaning joys enervate in the end,
But sorrow yields a glorious dividend
In the long run.

In the long run all hidden things are known,
The eye of truth will penetrate the night,
And good or ill, thy secret shall be known,
However well 'tis guarded from the light.
All the unspoken motives of the breast
Are fathomed by the years and stand confess'd
In the long run.

In the long run all love is paid by love,
Though undervalued by the hosts of earth;
The great eternal Government above
Keeps strict account and will redeem its worth.
Give thy love freely; do not count the cost;
So beautiful a thing was never lost
In the long run.

AS YOU GO THROUGH LIFE

Don't look for the flaws as you go through life;
And even when you find them,
It is wise and kind to be somewhat blind,
And look for the virtue behind them;
For the cloudiest night has a hint of light
Somewhere in its shadows hiding;
It's better by far to hunt for a star,
Than the spots on the sun abiding.

The current of life runs ever away
To the bosom of God's great ocean.
Don't set your force 'gainst the river's course,
And think to alter its motion.
Don't waste a curse on the universe,
Remember, it lived before you;
Don't butt at the storm with your puny form,
But bend and let it go o'er you.

The world will never adjust itself
To suit your whims to the letter,
Some things must go wrong your whole life long,

And the sooner you know it the better.
It is folly to fight with the Infinite,
And go under at last in the wrestle.
The wiser man shapes into God's plan,
As water shapes into a vessel.

TWO SUNSETS

In the fair morning of his life,
When his pure heart lay in his breast,
Panting, with all that wild unrest
To plunge into the great world's strife

That fills young hearts with mad desire,
He saw a sunset. Red and gold
The burning billows surged and rolled,
And upward tossed their caps of fire.

He looked. And as he looked, the sight
Sent from his soul through breast and brain
Such intense joy, it hurt like pain.
His heart seemed bursting with delight.

So near the Unknown seemed, so close
He might have grasped it with his hands
He felt his inmost soul expand,
As sunlight will expand a rose

One day he heard a singing strain
A human voice, in bird-like trills.
He paused, and little rapture-rills
Went trickling downward through each vein.

And in his heart the whole day long,
As in a temple veiled and dim,
He kept and bore about with him
The beauty of that singer's song.

And then? But why relate what then?
His smouldering heart flamed into fire
He had his one supreme desire,
And plunged into the world of men.

For years queen Folly held her sway.
With pleasures of the grosser kind
She fed his flesh and drugged his mind,
Till, shamed, he sated, turned away.

He sought his boyhood's home.
That hour Triumphant should have been, in sooth,
Since he went forth, an unknown youth,
And came back crowned with wealth and power.

The clouds made day a gorgeous bed;
He saw the splendour of the sky
With unmoved heart and stolid eye;
He only knew the West was red.

Then suddenly a fresh young voice
Rose, bird-like, from some hidden place,
He did not even turn his face -
It struck him simply as a noise.

He trod the old paths up and down.
Their rich-hued leaves by Fall winds whirled
How dull they were, how dull the world
Dull even in the pulsing town.

O! worst of punishments, that brings
A blunting of all finer sense,
A loss of feelings keen, intense,
And dulls us to the higher things.

O! penalty most dire, most sure,
Swift following after gross delights,
That we no more see beauteous sights,
Or hear as hear the good and pure.

O! shape more hideous and more dread
Than Vengeance takes in creed-taught minds,
This certain doom that blunts and blinds,
And strikes the holiest feelings dead.

UNREST

In the youth of the year, when the birds were building,
When the green was showing on tree and hedge,
And the tenderest light of all lights was gilding
The world from zenith to outermost edge,
My soul grew sad and longingly lonely!
I sighed for the season of sun and rose,
And I said, "In the Summer and that time only
Lies sweet contentment and blest repose."

With bee and bird for her maids of honour
Came Princess Summer in robes of green.
And the King of day smiled down upon her
And wooed her, and won her, and made her queen.
Fruit of their union and true love's pledges,
Beautiful roses bloomed day by day,
And rambled in gardens and hid in hedges
Like royal children in sportive play.

My restless soul for a little season
Revelled in rapture of glow and bloom,
And then, like a subject who harbours treason,
Grew full of rebellion and grey with gloom.
And I said, "I am sick of the summer's blisses,
Of warmth and beauty, and nothing more.
The full fruition my sad soul misses
That beauteous Fall-time holds in store!"

But now when the colours are almost blinding,
Burning and blending on bush and tree,
And the rarest fruits are mine for the finding,
And the year is ripe as a year can be,
My soul complains in the same old fashion;
Crying aloud in my troubled breast
Is the same old longing, the same old passion.
O where is the treasure which men call rest?

"ARTIST'S LIFE"

Of all the waltzes the great Strauss wrote,
Mad with melody, rhythm, rife
From the very first to the final note.
Give me his "Artist's Life!"

It stirs my blood to my finger-ends,
Thrills me and fills me with vague unrest,
And all that is sweetest and saddest blends
Together within my breast.

It brings back that night in the dim arcade,
In love's sweet morning and life's best prime,
When the great brass orchestra played and played,
And set our thoughts to rhyme.

It brings back that Winter of mad delights,
Of leaping pulses and tripping feet,
And those languid moon-washed Summer nights

When we heard the band in the street.

It brings back rapture and glee and glow,
It brings back passion and pain and strife,
And so of all the waltzes I know,
Give me the "Artist's Life."

For it is so full of the dear old time
So full of the dear old friends I knew.
And under its rhythm, and lilt, and rhyme,
I am always finding YOU.

NOTHING BUT STONES
I think I never passed so sad an hour,
Dear friend, as that one at the church to-night.
The edifice from basement to the tower
Was one resplendent blaze of coloured light.
Up through broad aisles the stylish crowd was thronging,
Each richly robed like some king's bidden guest.
"Here will I bring my sorrow and my longing,"
I said, "and here find rest."

I heard the heavenly organ's voice of thunder,
It seemed to give me infinite relief.
I wept. Strange eyes looked on in well-bred wonder.
I dried my tears: their gaze profaned my grief.
Wrapt in the costly furs, and silks, and laces,
Beat alien hearts, that had no part with me.
I could not read, in all those proud cold faces,
One thought of sympathy.

I watched them bowing and devoutly kneeling,
Heard their responses like sweet waters roll
But only the glorious organ's sacred pealing
Seemed gushing from a full and fervent soul.
I listened to the man of holy calling,
He spoke of creeds, and hailed his own as best;
Of man's corruption and of Adam's-falling,
But naught that gave me rest:

Nothing that helped me bear the daily grinding
Of soul with body, heart with heated brain;
Nothing to show the purpose of this blinding
And sometimes overwhelming sense of pain.
And then, dear friend, I thought of thee, so lowly,
So unassuming, and so gently kind,

And lo! a peace, a calm serene and holy,
Settled upon my mind.

Ah, friend, my friend! one true heart, fond and tender,
That understands our troubles and our needs,
Brings us more near to God than all the splendour
And pomp of seeming worship and vain creeds.
One glance of thy dear eyes so full of feeling,
Doth bring me closer to the Infinite
Than all that throng of worldly people kneeling
In blaze of gorgeous light.

INEVITABLE

To-day I was so weary and I lay
In that delicious state of semi-waking,
When baby, sitting with his nurse at play,
Cried loud for "mamma," all his toys forsaking.

I was so weary and I needed rest,
And signed to nurse to bear him from the room.
Then, sudden, rose and caught him to my breast,
And kissed the grieving mouth and cheeks of bloom.

For swift as lightning came the thought to me,
With pulsing heart-throes and a mist of tears,
Of days inevitable, that are to be,
If my fair darling grows to manhood's years;

Days when he will not call for "mamma," when
The world, with many a pleasure and bright joy,
Shall tempt him forth into the haunts of men
And I shall lose the first place with my boy;

When other homes and loves shall give delight,
When younger smiles and voices will seem best.
And so I held him to my heart to-night,
Forgetting all my need of peace and rest.

THE OCEAN OF SONG

In a land beyond sight or conceiving,
In a land where no blight is, no wrong,
No darkness, no graves, and no grieving,
There lies the great ocean of song.
And its waves, oh, its waves unbeholden
By any save gods, and their kind,

Are not blue, are not green, but are golden,
Like moonlight and sunlight combined.

It was whispered to me that their waters
Were made from the gathered-up tears
That were wept by the sons and the daughters
Of long-vanished eras and spheres.
Like white sands of heaven the spray is
That falls all the happy day long,
And whoever it touches straightway is
Made glad with the spirit of song.

Up, up to the clouds where their hoary
Crowned heads melt away in the skies,
The beautiful mountains of glory
Each side of the song-ocean rise.
Here day is one splendour of sky-light
Of God's light with beauty replete.
Here night is not night, but is twilight,
Pervading, enfolding, and sweet.

Bright birds from all climes and all regions,
That sing the whole glad summer long,
Are dumb, till they flock here in legions
And lave in the ocean of song.
It is here that the four winds of heaven,
The winds that do sing and rejoice,
It is here they first came and were given
The secret of sound and a voice.

Far down along beautiful beeches,
By night and by glorious day,
The throng of the gifted ones reaches,
Their foreheads made white with the spray,
And a few of the sons and the daughters
Of this kingdom, cloud-hidden from sight,
Go down in the wonderful waters,
And bathe in those billows of light.

And their souls evermore are like fountains,
And liquid and lucent and strong,
High over the tops of the mountains
Gush up the sweet billows of song.
No drouth-time of waters can dry them.
Whoever has bathed in that sea,
All dangers, all deaths, they defy them,
And are gladder than gods are, with glee.

"IT MIGHT HAVE BEEN"

We will be what we could be. Do not say,
"It might have been, had not or that, or this."
No fate can keep us from the chosen way;
He only might, who IS.

We will do what we could do. Do not dream
Chance leaves a hero, all uncrowned to grieve.
I hold, all men are greatly what they seem;
He does, who could achieve.

We will climb where we could climb. Tell me not
Of adverse storms that kept thee from the height.
What eagle ever missed the peak he sought?
He always climbs who might.

I do not like the phrase, "It might have been!"
It lacks all force, and life's best truths perverts
For I believe we have, and reach, and win,
Whatever our deserts.

MOMUS, GOD OF LAUGHTER

Though with gods the world is cumbered,
Gods unnamed, and gods unnumbered,
Never god was known to be
Who had not his devotee.
So I dedicate to mine,
Here in verse, my temple-shrine.

'Tis not Ares, mighty Mars,
Who can give success in wars.
'Tis not Morpheus, who doth keep
Guard above us while we sleep,
'Tis not Venus, she whose duty
'Tis to give us love and beauty;
Hail to these, and others, after
Momus, gleesome god of laughter.

Quirinus would guard my health,
Plutus would insure me wealth;
Mercury looks after trade,
Hera smiles on youth and maid.
All are kind, I own their worth,
After Momus, god of mirth.

Though Apollo, out of spite,
Hides away his face of light,
Though Minerva looks askance,
Deigning me no smiling glance,
Kings and queens may envy me
While I claim the god of glee.

Wisdom wearies, Love has wings
Wealth makes burdens, Pleasure stings,
Glory proves a thorny crown
So all gifts the gods throw down
Bring their pains and troubles after;
All save Momus, god of laughter.
He alone gives constant joy.
Hail to Momus, happy boy.

I DREAM

Oh, I have dreams. I sometimes dream of Life
In the full meaning of that splendid word.
Its subtle music which few men have heard,
Though all may hear it, sounding through earth's strife.
Its mountain heights by mystic breezes kissed
Lifting their lovely peaks above the dust;
Its treasures which no touch of time can rust,
Its emerald seas, its dawns of amethyst,
Its certain purpose, its serene repose,
Its usefulness, that finds no hour for woes,
This is my dream of Life.

Yes, I have dreams. I ofttimes dream of Love
As radiant and brilliant as a star.
As changeless, too, as that fixed light afar
Which glorifies vast worlds of space above.
Strong as the tempest when it holds its breath,
Before it bursts in fury; and as deep
As the unfathomed seas, where lost worlds sleep,
And sad as birth, and beautiful as death.
As fervent as the fondest soul could crave,
Yet holy as the moonlight on a grave.
This is my dream of Love.

Yes, yes, I dream. One oft-recurring dream
Is beautiful and comforting and blest,
Complete with certain promises of rest,
Divine content, and ecstasy supreme.

When that strange essence, author of all faith,
That subtle something, which cries for the light,
Like a lost child who wanders in the night,
Shall solve the mighty mystery of Death,
Shall find eternal progress, or sublime
And satisfying slumber for all time.
This is my dream of Death.

THE SONNET
Alone it stands in Poesy's fair land,
A temple by the muses set apart;
A perfect structure of consummate art,
By artists builded and by genius planned,
Beyond the reach of the apprentice hand,
Beyond the ken of the untutored heart,
Like a fine carving in a common mart,
Only the favoured few will understand.
A chef d'auvre toiled over with great care,
Yet which the unseeing careless crowd goes by,
A plainly set, but well-cut solitaire,
An ancient bit of pottery, too rare
To please or hold aught save the special eye,
These only with the sonnet can compare.

THE PAST
Fling my past behind me, like a robe
Worn threadbare in the seams, and out of date.
I have outgrown it. Wherefore should I weep
And dwell up on its beauty, and its dyes
Of Oriental splendour, or complain
That I must needs discard it? I can weave
Upon the shuttles of the future years
A fabric far more durable. Subdued,
It may be, in the blending of its hues,
Where sombre shades commingle, yet the gleam
Of golden warp shall shoot it through and through,
While over all a fadeless lustre lies,
And starred with gems made out of crystalled tears,
My new robe shall be richer than the old.

A DREAM
That was a curious dream; I thought the three
Great planets that are drawing near the sun
With such unerring certainty begun

To talk together in a mighty glee.
They spoke of vast convulsions which would be
Throughout the solar system the rare fun
Of watching haughty stars drop, one by one,
And vanish in a seething vapour sea.

I thought I heard them comment on the earth
That small dark object, doomed beyond a doubt.
They wondered if live creatures moved about
Its tiny surface, deeming it of worth.
And then they laughed, 'twas such a singing shout
That I awoke and joined too in their mirth.

USELESSNESS

Let mine not be that saddest fate of all
To live beyond my greater self; to see
My faculties decaying, as the tree
Stands stark and helpless while its green leaves fall.
Let me hear rather the imperious call,
Which all men dread, in my glad morning time,
And follow death ere I have reached my prime,
Or drunk the strengthening cordial of life's gall.
The lightning's stroke or the fierce tempest blast
Which fells the green tree to the earth to-day
Is kinder than the calm that lets it last,
Unhappy witness of its own decay.
May no man ever look on me and say,
"She lives, but all her usefulness is past."

WILL

There is no chance, no destiny, no fate,
Can circumvent or hinder or control
The firm resolve of a determined soul.
Gifts count for nothing; will alone is great;
All things give way before it, soon or late.
What obstacle can stay the mighty force
Of the sea-seeking river in its course,
Or cause the ascending orb of day to wait?

Each well-born soul must win what it deserves.
Let the fool prate of luck. The fortunate
Is he whose earnest purpose never swerves,
Whose slightest action or inaction serve.
The one great aim.
Why, even Death stands still,

And waits an hour sometimes for such a will.

WINTER RAIN

Falling upon the frozen world last
I heard the slow beat of the Winter rain
Poor foolish drops, down-dripping all in vain;
The ice-bound Earth but mocked their puny might,
Far better had the fixedness of white
And uncomplaining snows, which make no sign,
But coldly smile, when pitying moonbeams shine
Concealed its sorrow from all human sight.
Long, long ago, in blurred and burdened years,
I learned the uselessness of uttered woe.
Though sinewy Fate deals her most skilful blow,
I do not waste the gall now of my tears,
But feed my pride upon its bitter, while
I look straight in the world's bold eyes, and smile.

LIFE

Life, like a romping schoolboy, full of glee,
Doth bear us on his shoulder for a time.
There is no path too steep for him to climb.
With strong, lithe limbs, as agile and as free,
As some young roe, he speeds by vale and sea,
By flowery mead, by mountain peak sublime,
And all the world seems motion set to rhyme,
Till, tired out, he cries, "Now carry me!"
In vain we murmur; "Come," Life says, "Fair play!"
And seizes on us. God! he goads us so!
He does not let us sit down all the day.
At each new step we feel the burden grow,
Till our bent backs seem breaking as we go,
Watching for Death to meet us on the way.

BURDENED

"Genius, a man's weapon, a woman's burden." - Lamartine.

Dear God! there is no sadder fate in life
Than to be burdened so that you can not
Sit down contented with the common lot
Of happy mother and devoted wife.

To feel your brain wild and your bosom rife
With all the sea's commotion; to be fraught

With fires and frenzies which you have not sought,
And weighed down with the wild world's weary strife;

To feel a fever always in your breast;
To lean and hear, half in affright, half shame,
A loud-voiced public boldly mouth your name;
To reap your hard-sown harvest in unrest,
And know, however great your meed of fame,
You are but a weak woman at the best.

LET THEM GO

Let the dream go. Are there not other dreams
In vastness of clouds hid from thy sight
That yet shall gild with beautiful gold gleams,
And shoot the shadows through and through with light?
What matters one lost vision of the night?
Let the dream go!!

Let the hope set. Are there not other hopes
That yet shall rise like new stars in thy sky?
Not long a soul in sullen darkness gropes
Before some light is lent it from on high;
What folly to think happiness gone by!
Let the hope set!

Let the joy fade. Are there not other joys,
Like frost-bound bulbs, that yet shall start and bloom?
Severe must be the winter that destroys
The hardy roots locked in their silent tomb.
What cares the earth for her brief time of gloom
Let the joy fade!

Let the love die. Are there not other loves
As beautiful and full of sweet unrest,
Flying through space like snowy-pinioned doves?
They yet shall come and nestle in thy breast,
And thou shalt say of each, "Lo, this is best!"
Let the love die!

FIVE KISSES

I - THE MOTHER'S KISS

Love breathed a secret to her listening heart,
And said "Be silent." Though she guarded it,
And dwelt as one within a world apart,

Yet sun and star seemed by that secret lit.
And where she passed, each whispering wind ablow,
And every little blossom in the sod,
Called joyously to her, "We know, we know,
For are we not the intimates of God?"
Life grew so radiant, and so opulent,
That when her fragile body and her brain
By mortal throes of agony were rent,
She felt a curious rapture in her pain.
Then, after anguish, came the supreme bliss
They brought the little baby, for her kiss!

II - THE BETROTHAL
There was a little pause between the dances;
Without, somewhere, a tinkling fountain played.
The dusky path was lit by ardent glances
As forth they fared, a lover and a maid.
He chose a nook, from curious eyes well hidden
All redolent with sweet midsummer charm,
And by the great primeval instinct bidden,
He drew her in the shelter of his arm.
The words that long deep in his heart had trembled
Found sudden utterance; she at first dissembled,
Refused her lips, and half withdrew her hand,
Then murmured "Yes," and yielded, woman fashion,
Her virgin mouth to young love's kiss of passion.

III - THE BRIDAL KISS
As fleecy clouds trail back across the skies,
Showing the sweet young moon in azure space,
The lifted veil revealed her shining face
A sudden wonder to his eager eyes.
In that familiar beauty lurked surprise:
For now the wife stood in the maiden's place
With conscious dignity, and woman's grace,
And love's large pride grown trebly fair and wise.

The world receded, leaving them alone.
The universe was theirs, from sphere to sphere,
And life assumed new meaning, and new worth.
Love held no privilege they did not own,
And when they kissed each other without fear,
They understood why God had made the earth.

IV - DOMESTIC BLISS
Sequestered in their calm domestic bower,
They sat together. He in manhood's prime

And she a matron in her fullest flower.
The mantel clock gave forth a warning chime.
She put her work aside; his bright cigar
Grew pale, and crumbled in an ashen heap.
The lights went out, save one remaining star
That watched beside the children in their sleep.
She hummed a little song and nestled near,
As side by side they went to their repose.
His arm about her waist, he whispered "Dear,"
And pressed his lips upon her mouth's full rose
The sacred sweetness of their wedded life
Breathed in that kiss of husband and of wife.

V - OLD AGE
The young see heaven but to the old who wait
The final call, the hills of youth arise
More beautiful than shores of Paradise.
Beside a glowing and voracious grate
A dozing couple dream of yesterday;
The islands of a vanished past appear,
Bringing forgotten names and faces near;
While lost in mist, the present fades away.
The fragrant winds of tender memories blow
Across the gardens of the "Used-to-be!"
They smile into each other's eyes, and see
The bride and bridegroom of the long ago.
And tremulous lips, pressed close to faded cheek
Love's silent tale of deathless passion speak.

RETROSPECTION
I look down the lengthening distance
Far back to youth's valley of hope.
How strange seemed the ways of existence,
How infinite life and its scope!

What dreams, what ambitions came thronging
To people a world of my own!
How the heart in my bosom was longing,
For pleasures and places unknown.

But the hill-tops of pleasure and beauty
Were covered with mist at the dawn;
And only the rugged road Duty
Shone clear, as my feet wandered on.

I loved not the path and its leading,

I hated the rocks and the dust;
But a Voice from the Silence was pleading,
It spoke but one syllable "Trust."

I saw, as the morning grew older,
The fair flowered hills of delight;
And the feet of my comrades grew bolder,
They hurried away from my sight.

And when on the pathway I faltered,
And when I rebelled at my fate,
The Voice with assurance unaltered,
Again spoke one syllable "Wait."

Along the hard highway I travelled
And saw, with dim vision, how soon
The morning's gold locks were unravelled,
By fingers of amorous noon.

A turn in the pathway of duty
I stood in the perfect day's prime,
Close, close to the hillside of beauty
The Voice from the Silence said "Climb"

The road to the beautiful Regions
Lies ever through Duty's hard way.
Oh ye who go searching in legions,
Know this and be patient to-day.

HELENA

Last night I saw Helena. She whose praise
Of late all men have sounded. She for whom
Young Angus rashly sought a silent tomb
Rather than live without her all his days.

Wise men go mad who look upon her long,
She is so ripe with dangers. Yet meanwhile
I find no fascination in her smile,
Although I make her theme of this poor song.

"Her golden tresses?" yes, they may be fair,
And yet to me each shining silken tress
Seems robbed of beauty and all lustreless
Too many hands have stroked Helena's hair.

(I know a little maiden so demure

She will not let her one true lover's hands
In playful fondness touch her soft brown bands
So dainty-minded is she, and so pure.)

"Her great dark eyes that flash like gems at night?
Large, long-lashed eyes and lustrous?" that may be,
And yet they are not beautiful to me.
Too many hearts have sunned in their delight.

(I mind me of two tender blue eyes, hid
So underneath white curtains, and so veiled
That I have sometimes plead for hours, and failed
To see more than the shyly lifted lid.)

"Her perfect mouth so liked a carved kiss?"
"Her honeyed-mouth, where hearts do, fly-like, drown?"
I would not taste its sweetness for a crown;
Too many lips have drank its nectared bliss.

(I know a mouth whose virgin dew, undried,
Lies like a young grape's bloom, untouched and sweet,
And though I plead in passion at her feet,
She would not let me brush it if I died.)

In vain, Helena! though wise men may vie
For thy rare smile, or die from loss of it,
Armoured by my sweet lady's trust, I sit,
And know thou are not worth her faintest sigh.

NOTHING REMAINS

Nothing remains of unrecorded ages
That lie in the silent cemetery time;
Their wisdom may have shamed our wisest sages,
Their glory may have been indeed sublime.
How weak do seem our strivings after power,
How poor the grandest efforts of our brains,
If out of all we are, in one short hour
Nothing remains.

Nothing remains but the Eternal Spaces,
Time and decay uproot the forest trees.
Even the mighty mountains leave their places,
And sink their haughty heads beneath strange seas
The great earth writhes in some convulsive spasms
And turns the proudest cities into plains.
The level sea becomes a yawning chasm

Nothing remains.

Nothing remains but the Eternal Forces,
The sad seas cease complaining and grow dry,
Rivers are drained and altered in their courses,
Great stars pass out and vanish from the sky.
Ideas die and old religions perish,
Our rarest pleasures and our keenest pains
Are swept away with all we hate or cherish
Nothing remains.

Nothing remains but the Eternal Nameless
And all-creative spirit of the Law,
Uncomprehended, comprehensive, blameless,
Invincible, resistless, with no flaw;
So full of love it must create forever,
Destroying that it may create again,
Persistent and perfecting in endeavour,
It yet must bring forth angels, after men
This, this remains!

COMRADES

I and my Soul are alone to-day,
All in the shining weather;
We were sick of the world, and put it away,
So we could rejoice together.

Our host, the Sun, in the blue, blue sky
Is mixing a rare, sweet wine,
In the burnished gold of this cup on high,
For me, and this Soul of mine.

We find it a safe and royal drink,
And a cure for every pain;
It helps us to love, and helps us to think,
And strengthens body and brain.

And sitting here, with my Soul alone,
Where the yellow sun-rays fall,
Of all the friends I have ever known
I find it the BEST of all.

We rarely meet when the world is near,
For the World hath a pleasing art
And brings me so much that is bright and dear
That my Soul it keepeth apart.

But when I grow weary of mirth and glee,
Of glitter, glow, and splendour,
Like a tried old friend it comes to me,
With a smile that is sad and tender.

And we walk together as two friends may,
And laugh and drink God's wine.
Oh, a royal comrade any day
I find this Soul of mine.

WHAT GAIN?

Now, while thy rounded cheek is fresh and fair,
While beauty lingers, laughing, in thine eyes,
Ere thy young heart shall meet the stranger, "Care,"
Or thy blithe soul become the home of sighs,
Were it not kindness should I give thee rest
By plunging this sharp dagger in thy breast?
Dying so young, with all thy wealth of youth,
What part of life wouldst thou not claim, in sooth?
Only the woe,
Sweetheart, that sad souls know.

Now, in this sacred hour of supreme trust,
Of pure delight and palpitating joy,
Ere change can come, as come it surely must,
With jarring doubts and discords, to destroy
Our far too perfect peace, I pray thee, Sweet,
Were it not best for both of us, and meet,
If I should bring swift death to seal our bliss?
Dying so full of joy, what could we miss?
Nothing but tears,
Sweetheart, and weary years.

How slight the action! Just one well-aimed blow
Here, where I feel thy warm heart's pulsing beat,
And then another through my own, and so
Our perfect union would be made complete:
So, past all parting, I should claim thee mine.
Dead with our youth, and faith, and love divine,
Should we not keep the best of life that way?
What shall we gain by living day on day?
What shall we gain,
Sweetheart, but bitter pain?

TO THE WEST

Not to the crowded East,
Where, in a well-worn groove,
Like the harnessed wheel of a great machine,
The trammelled mind must move
Where Thought must follow the fashion of Thought,
Or be counted vulgar and set at naught.

Not to the languid South,
Where the mariners of the brain
Are lured by the Sirens of the Sense,
And wrecked upon its main
Where Thought is rocked, on the sweet wind's breath
To a torpid sleep that ends in death.

But to the mighty West,
That chosen realm of God,
Where Nature reaches her hands to men,
And Freedom walks abroad
Where mind is King, and fashion is naught,
There shall the New World look for thought

To the West, the beautiful West,
She shall look, and not in vain
For out of its broad and boundless store
Come muscle, and nerve, and brain.
Let the bards of the East and the South be dumb
For out of the West shall the Poets come.

They shall come with souls as great
As the cradle where they were rocked;
They shall come with brows that are touched with fire
Like the gods with whom they have walked;
They shall come from the West in royal state,
The Singers and Thinkers for whom we wait.

THE LAND OF CONTENT

I set out for the Land of Content,
By the gay crowded pleasure-highway,
With laughter, and jesting, I went
With the mirth-loving throng for a day;
Then I knew I had wandered astray,
For I met returned pilgrims, belated,
Who said, "We are weary and sated,
But we found not the Land of Content."

I turned to the steep path of fame,
I said, "It is over yon height
This land with the beautiful name
Ambition will lend me its light."
But I paused in my journey ere night,
For the way grew so lonely and troubled;
I said my anxiety doubled
"This is not the road to Content."

Then I joined the great rabble and throng
That frequents the moneyed world's mart;
But the greed, and the grasping and wrong,
Left me only one wish, to depart.
And sickened, and saddened at heart,
I hurried away from the gateway,
For my soul and my spirit said straightway.
"This is not the road to Content."

Then weary in body and brain,
An overgrown path I detected,
And I said "I will hide with my pain
In this byway, unused and neglected."
Lo! it led to the realm God selected
To crown with His best gifts of beauty,
And through the dark pathway of duty
I came to the land of Content.

WARNING
High in the heavens I saw the moon this morning,
Albeit the sun shone bright;
Unto my soul it spoke, in voice of warning,
"Remember Night!"

AFTER THE BATTLES ARE OVER
After the battles are over,
And the war drums cease to beat,
And no more is heard on the hillside
The sound of hurrying feet,
Full many a noble action,
That was done in the days of strife
By the soldier is half forgotten,
In the peaceful walks of life.

Just as the tangled grasses,
In Summer's warmth and light,

Grow over the graves of the fallen
And hide them away from sight,
So many an act of valour,
And many a deed sublime,
Fade from the mind of the soldier
O'ergrown by the grass of time

Not so should they be rewarded,
Those noble deeds of old!
They should live forever and ever,
When the heroes' hearts are cold.
Then rally, ye brave old comrades,
Old veterans, reunite!
Uproot Time's tangled grasses
Live over the march, and the fight.

Let Grant come up from the White House,
And clasp each brother's hand,
First chieftain of the army,
Last chieftain of the land.
Let him rest from a nation's burdens,
And go, in thought, with his men,
Through the fire and smoke of Shiloh,
And save the day again.

This silent hero of battles
Knew no such word as defeat.
It was left for the rebels' learning,
Along with the word, retreat.
He was not given to talking,
But he found that guns would preach
In a way that was more convincing
Than fine and flowery speech

Three cheers for the grave commander
Of the grand old Tennessee!
Who won the first great battle
Gained the first great victory.
His motto was always "Conquer,"
"Success" was his countersign,
And "though it took all Summer,"
He kept fighting upon "that line."

Let Sherman, the stern old General,
Come rallying with his men;
Let them march once more through Georgia
And down to the sea again.

Oh! that grand old tramp to Savannah,
Three hundred miles to the coast,
It will live in the heart of the nation,
For ever its pride and boast.

As Sheridan went to the battle,
When a score of miles away,
He has come to the feast and banquet,
By the iron horse to-day.
Its pace is not much swifter
Than the pace of that famous steed
Which bore him down to the contest
And saved the day by his speed.

Then go over the ground to-day, boys
Tread each remembered spot.
It will be a gleesome journey,
On the swift-shod feet of thought;
You can fight a bloodless battle,
You can skirmish along the route,
But it's not worth while to forage,
There are rations enough without.

Don't start if you hear the cannon,
It is not the sound of doom,
It does not call to the contest
To the battle's smoke and gloom.
"Let us have peace," was spoken,
And lo! peace ruled again;
And now the nation is shouting,
Through the cannon's voice, "Amen."

O boys who besieged old Vicksburgh,
Can time e'er wash away
The triumph of her surrender,
Nine years ago to-day?
Can you ever forget the moment,
When you saw the flag of white,
That told how the grim old city
Had fallen in her might?

Ah, 'twas a bold, brave army,
When the boys, with a right good will,
Went gally marching and singing
To the fight at Champion Hill.
They met with a warm reception,
But the soul of "Old John Brown"

Was abroad on that field of battle,
And our flag did NOT go down.

Come, heroes of Look Out Mountain,
Of Corinth and Donelson,
Of Kenesaw and Atlanta,
And tell how the day was won!
Hush! bow the head for a moment
There are those who cannot come.
No bugle-call can arouse them
No sound of fife or drum.

Oh, boys who died for the country,
Oh, dear and sainted dead!
What can we say about you
That has not once been said?
Whether you fell in the contest,
Struck down by shot and shell,
Or pined 'neath the hand of sickness
Or starved in the prison cell,

We know that you died for Freedom,
To save our land from shame,
To rescue a perilled Nation,
And we give you deathless fame.
'Twas the cause of Truth and Justice
That you fought and perished for,
And we say it, oh, so gently,
"Our boys who died in the war."

Saviours of our Republic,
Heroes who wore the blue,
We owe the peace that surrounds us
And our Nation's strength to you.
We owe it to you that our banner,
The fairest flag in the world,
Is to-day unstained, unsullied,
On the Summer air unfurled.

We look on its stripes and spangles,
And our hearts are filled the while
With love for the brave commanders,
And the boys of the rank and file.
The grandest deeds of valour
Were never written out,
The noblest acts of virtue
The world knows nothing about.

And many a private soldier,
Who walks his humble way,
With no sounding name or title,
Unknown to the world to-day,
In the eyes of God is a hero
As worthy of the bays
As any mighty General
To whom the world gives praise.

Brave men of a mighty army,
We extend you friendship's hand
I speak for the "Loyal Women,"
Those pillars of our land.
We wish you a hearty welcome,
We are proud that you gather here
To talk of old times together
On this brightest day in the year.

And if Peace, whose snow-white pinions
Brood over our land to-day,
Should ever again go from us,
(God grant she may ever stay!)
Should our Nation call in her peril
For "Six hundred thousand more,"
The loyal women would hear her,
And send you out as before.

We would bring out the treasured knapsack,
We would take the sword from the wall,
And hushing our own hearts' pleadings,
Hear only the country's call.
For next to our God is our Nation;
And we cherish the honoured name
Of the bravest of all brave armies
Who fought for that Nation's fame.

AND THEY ARE DUMB
I have been across the bridges of the years.
Wet with tears
Were the ties on which I trod, going back
Down the track
To the valley where I left, 'neath skies of Truth,
My lost youth.

As I went, I dropped my burdens, one and all

Let them fall;
All my sorrows, all my wrinkles, all my care,
My white hair,
I laid down, like some lone pilgrim's heavy pack,
By the track.

As I neared the happy valley with light feet,
My heart beat
To the rhythm of a song I used to know
Long ago,
And my spirits gushed and bubbled like a fountain
Down a mountain.

On the border of that valley I found you,
Tried and true;
And we wandered through the golden Summer-Land
Hand in hand.
And my pulses beat with rapture in the blisses
Of your kisses.

And we met there, in those green and verdant places,
Smiling faces,
And sweet laughter echoed upward from the dells
Like gold bells.
And the world was spilling over with the glory
Of Youth's story.

It was but a dreamer's journey of the brain;
And again
I have left the happy valley far behind;
And I find
Time stands waiting with his burdens in a pack
For my back.

As he speeds me, like a rough, well-meaning friend,
To the end,
Will I find again the lost ones loved so well?
Who can tell!
But the dead know what the life will be to come
And they are dumb!

NIGHT
As some dusk mother shields from all alarms
The tired child she gathers to her breast,
The brunette Night doth fold me in her arms,
And hushes me to perfect peace and rest.

Her eyes of stars shine on me, and I hear
Her voice of winds low crooning on my ear.
O Night, O Night, how beautiful thou art!
Come, fold me closer to thy pulsing heart.

The day is full of gladness, and the light
So beautifies the common outer things,
I only see with my external sight,
And only hear the great world's voice which rings.
But silently from daylight and from din
The sweet Night draws me, whispers, "Look within!"
And looking, as one wakened from a dream,
I see what IS, no longer what doth seem.

The Night says, "Listen!" and upon my ear
Revealed, as are the visions to my sight,
The voices known as "Beautiful" come near
And whisper of the vastly Infinite.
Great, blue-eyed Truth, her sister Purity,
Their brother Honour, all converse with me,
And kiss my brow, and say, "Be brave of heart!"
O holy three! how beautiful thou art!

The Night says, "Child, sleep that thou may'st arise
Strong for to-morrow's struggle." And I feel
Her shadowy fingers pressing on my eyes:
Like thistledown I float to the Ideal
The Slumberland, made beautiful and bright
As death, by dreams of loved ones gone from sight,
O food for souls, sweet dreams of pure delight,
How beautiful the holy hours of Night!

ALL FOR ME
The world grows green on a thousand hills
By a thousand willows the bees are humming,
And a million birds by a million rills,
Sing of the golden season coming.
But, gazing out on the sun-kist lea,
And hearing a thrush and a blue-bird singing,
I feel that the summer is all for me,
And all for me are the joys it is bringing.

All for me the bumble-bee
Drones his song in the perfect weather;
And, just on purpose to sing to me,
Thrush and blue-bird came North together.

Just for me, in red and white,
Bloom and blossom the fields of clover;
And all for me and my delight
The wild Wind follows and plays the lover.

The mighty sun, with a scorching kiss
(I have read, and heard, and do not doubt it)
Has burned up a thousand worlds like this,
And never stopped to think about it.
And yet I believe he hurries up
Just on purpose to kiss my flowers
To drink the dew from the lily-cup,
And help it to grow through golden hours.

I know I am only a speck of dust,
An individual mite of masses,
Clinging upon the outer crust
Of a little ball of cooling gases.
And yet, and yet, say what you will,
And laugh, if you please, at my lack of reason,
For me wholly, and for me still,
Blooms and blossoms the Summer season.

Nobody else has ever heard
The story the Wind to me discloses;
And none but I and the humming-bird
Can read the hearts of the crimson roses.
Ah, my Summer, my love, my own!
The world grows glad in your smiling weather;
Yet all for me, and me alone,
You and your Court came North together.

INTO SPACE

If the sad old world should jump a cog
Sometime, in its dizzy spinning,
And go off the track with a sudden jog,
What an end would come to the sinning,
What a rest from strife and the burdens of life
For the millions of people in it,
What a way out of care, and worry and wear,
All in a beautiful minute.

As 'round the sun with a curving sweep
It hurries and runs and races,
Should it lose its balance, and go with a leap
Into the vast sea-spaces,

What a blest relief it would bring to the grief,
And the trouble and toil about us,
To be suddenly hurled from the solar world
And let it go on without us.

With not a sigh or a sad good-bye
For loved ones left behind us,
We would go with a lunge and a mighty plunge
Where never a grave should find us.
What a wild mad thrill our veins would fill
As the great earth, like a feather,
Should float through the air to God knows where,
And carry us all together.

No dark, damp tomb and no mourner's gloom,
No tolling bell in the steeple,
But in one swift breath a painless death
For a million billion people.
What greater bliss could we ask than this,
To sweep with a bird's free motion
Through leagues of space to a resting place,
In a vast and vapoury ocean -
To pass away from this life for aye
With never a dear tie sundered,
And a world on fire for a funeral pyre,
While the stars looked on and wondered?

THROUGH DIM EYES

Is it the world, or my eyes, that are sadder?
I see not the grace that I used to see
In the meadow-brook whose song was so glad, or
In the boughs of the willow tree.
The brook runs slower, its song seems lower
And not the song that it sang of old;
And the tree I admired looks weary and tired
Of the changeless story of heat and cold.

When the sun goes up, and the stars go under,
In that supreme hour of the breaking day,
Is it my eyes, or the dawn, I wonder,
That finds less of the gold, and more of the gray
I see not the splendour, the tints so tender,
The rose-hued glory I used to see;
And I often borrow a vague half-sorrow
That another morning has dawned for me.

When the royal smile of that welcome comer
Beams on the meadow and burns in the sky,
Is it my eyes, or does the Summer
Bring less of bloom than in days gone by?
The beauty that thrilled me, the rapture that filled me,
To an overflowing of happy tears,
I pass unseeing, my sad eyes being
Dimmed by the shadow of vanished years.

When the heart grows weary, all things seem dreary;
When the burden grows heavy, the way seems long.
Thank God for sending kind death as an ending,
Like a grand Amen to a minor song.

THE PUNISHED

Not they who know the awful gibbet's anguish,
Not they who, while sad years go by them, in
The sunless cells of lonely prisons languish,
Do suffer fullest penalty for sin.

'Tis they who walk the highways unsuspected,
Yet with grim fear for ever at their side,
Who hug the corpse of some sin undetected,
A corpse no grave or coffin-lid can hide

'Tis they who are in their own chambers haunted
By thoughts that like unbidden guests intrude,
And sit down, uninvited and unwanted,
And make a nightmare of the solitude.

HALF FLEDGED

I feel the stirrings in me of great things.
New half-fledged thoughts rise up and beat their wings,
And tremble on the margin of their nest,
Then flutter back, and hide within my breast.

Beholding space, they doubt their untried strength.
Beholding men, they fear them. But at length,
Grown all too great and active for the heart
That broods them with such tender mother art,
Forgetting fear, and men, and all, that hour,
Save the impelling consciousness of power
That stirs within them, they shall soar away
Up to the very portals of the Day.

Oh, what exultant rapture thrills me through
When I contemplate all those thoughts may do;
Like snow-white eagles penetrating space,
They may explore full many an unknown place,
And build their nests on mountain heights unseen,
Whereon doth lie that dreamed-of rest serene.
Stay thou a little longer in my breast,
Till my fond heart shall push thee from the nest
Anxious to see thee soar to heights divine
Oh, beautiful but half-fledged thoughts of mine.

THE YEAR
What can be said in New Year rhymes,
That's not been said a thousand times?

The new years come, the old years go,
We know we dream, we dream we know.

We rise up laughing with the light,
We lie down weeping with the night.

We hug the world until it stings,
We curse it then and sigh for wings.

We live, we love, we woo, we wed,
We wreathe our brides, we sheet our dead.

We laugh, we weep, we hope, we fear,
And that's the burden of the year.

THE UNATTAINED
A vision beauteous as the morn,
With heavenly eyes and tresses streaming,
Slow glided o'er a field late shorn
Where walked a poet idly dreaming.
He saw her, and joy lit his face,
"Oh, vanish not at human speaking,"
He cried, "thou form of magic grace,
Thou art the poem I am seeking.

"I've sought thee long! I claim thee now
My thought embodied, living, real."
She shook the tresses from her brow.
"Nay, nay!" she said, "I am ideal.
I am the phantom of desire -

The spirit of all great endeavour,
I am the voice that says, 'Come higher,'
That calls men up and up forever.

"'Tis not alone thy thought supreme
That here upon thy path has risen;
I am the artist's highest dream,
The ray of light he cannot prison.
I am the sweet ecstatic note
Than all glad music gladder, clearer,
That trembles in the singer's throat,
And dies without a human hearer.

"I am the greater, better yield,
That leads and cheers thy farmer neighbour,
For me he bravely tills the field
And whistles gaily at his labour.
Not thou alone, O poet soul,
Dost seek me through an endless morrow,
But to the toiling, hoping whole
I am at once the hope and sorrow.

"The spirit of the unattained,
I am to those who seek to name me,
A good desired but never gained:
All shall pursue, but none shall claim me."

IN THE CROWD
How happy they are, in all seeming,
How gay, or how smilingly proud,
How brightly their faces are beaming,
These people who make up the crowd!
How they bow, how they bend, how they flutter,
How they look at each other and smile,
How they glow, and what bon mots they utter!
But a strange thought has found me the while!

It is odd, but I stand here and fancy
These people who now play a part,
All forced by some strange necromancy
To speak, and to act, from the heart.
What a hush would come over the laughter!
What a silence would fall on the mirth!
And then what a wail would sweep after,
As the night-wind sweeps over the earth!

If the secrets held under and hidden
In the intricate hearts of the crowd
Were suddenly called to, and bidden
To rise up and cry out aloud,
How strange one would look to another!
Old friends of long standing and years
Own brothers would not know each other,
Robed new in their sorrows and fears.

From broadcloth, and velvet, and laces,
Would echo the groans of despair,
And there would be blanching of faces
And wringing of hands and of hair.
That man with his record of honour,
That lady down there with the rose,
That girl with Spring's freshness upon her,
Who knoweth the secrets of those?

Smile on, O ye maskers, smile sweetly!
Step lightly, bow low and laugh loud!
Though the world is deceived and completely,
I know ye, O sad-hearted crowd!
I watch you with infinite pity:
But play on, play ever your part,
Be gleeful, be joyful, be witty!
'Tis better than showing the heart.

LIFE AND I

Life and I are lovers, straying
Arm in arm along:
Often like two children Maying,
Full of mirth and song,

Life plucks all the blooming hours
Growing by the way;
Binds them on my brow like flowers,
Calls me Queen of May.

Then again, in rainy weather,
We sit vis-a-vis,
Planning work we'll do together
In the years to be.

Sometimes Life denies me blisses,
And I frown or pout;
But we make it up with kisses

Ere the day is out.

Woman-like, I sometimes grieve him,
Try his trust and faith,
Saying I shall one day leave him
For his rival, Death.

Then he always grows more zealous,
Tender, and more true;
Loves the more for being jealous,
As all lovers do.

Though I swear by stars above him,
And by worlds beyond,
That I love him, love him, love him;
Though my heart is fond;

Though he gives me, doth my lover,
Kisses with each breath
I shall one day throw him over,
And plight troth with Death.

GUERDON

Upon the white cheek of the Cherub Year
I saw a tear.
Alas! I murmured, that the Year should borrow
So soon a sorrow.
Just then the sunlight fell with sudden flame:
The tear became
A wondrous diamond sparkling in the light
A beauteous sight.

Upon my soul there fell such woeful loss,
I said, "The Cross
Is grievous for a life as young as mine."
Just then, like wine,
God's sunlight shone from His high Heavens down;
And lo! a crown
Gleamed in the place of what I thought a burden
My sorrow's guerdon.

SNOWED UNDER

Of a thousand things that the Year snowed under
The busy Old Year who has gone away
How many will rise in the Spring, I wonder,

Brought to life by the sun of May?
Will the rose-tree branches, so wholly hidden
That never a rose-tree seems to be,
At the sweet Spring's call come forth unbidden,
And bud in beauty, and bloom for me?

Will the fair green Earth, whose throbbing bosom
Is hid like a maid's in her gown at night,
Wake out of her sleep, and with blade and blossom
Gem her garments to please my sight?
Over the knoll in the valley yonder
The loveliest buttercups bloomed and grew;
When the snow has gone that drifted them under,
Will they shoot up sunward, and bloom anew?

When wild winds blew, and a sleet-storm pelted,
I lost a jewel of priceless worth;
If I walk that way when snows have melted,
Will the gem gleam up from the bare brown Earth?
I laid a love that was dead or dying,
For the year to bury and hide from sight;
But out of a trance will it waken, crying,
And push to my heart, like a leaf to the light?

Under the snow lie things so cherished
Hopes, ambitions, and dreams of men
Faces that vanished, and trusts that perished,
Never to sparkle and glow again.
The Old Year greedily grasped his plunder,
And covered it over and hurried away:
Of the thousand things that he did, I wonder
How many will rise at the call of May?
O wise Young Year, with your hands held under
Your mantle of ermine, tell me, pray!

"LEUDEMANNS-ON-THE-RIVER."
Toward even, when the day leans down
To kiss the upturned face of night,
Out just beyond the loud-voiced town
I know a spot of calm delight.
Like crimson arrows from a quiver
The red rays pierce the waters flowing,
While we go dreaming, singing, rowing
To Leudemanns-on the River.

The hills, like some glad mocking-bird,

Send back our laughter and our singing,
While faint, and yet more faint is heard
The steeple bells all sweetly ringing.
Some message did the winds deliver
To each glad heart that August night,
All heard, but all heard not aright,
By Leudemanns-on-the-River.

Night falls as in some foreign clime,
Between the hills that slope and rise.
So dusk the shades at landing-time,
We could not see each other's eyes.
We only saw the moonbeams quiver
Far down upon the stream! that night
The new moon gave but little light
By Leudemanns-on-the-River.

How dusky were those paths that led
Up from the river to the hall.
The tall trees branching overhead
Invite the early shades that fall.
In all the glad blithe world, oh, never
Were hearts more free from care than when
We wandered through those walks, we ten,
By Leudemanns-on-the-River.

So soon, so soon, the changes came.
This August day we two alone,
On that same river, not the same,
Dream of a night for ever flown.
Strange distances have come to sever
The hearts that gaily beat in pleasure,
Long miles we cannot cross or measure
From Leudemanns-on-the-River.

We'll pluck two leaves, dear friend, to-day.
The green, the russet! seems it strange
So soon, so soon, the leaves can change!
Ah me! so runs all life away.
This night-wind chills me, and I shiver;
The Summer-time is almost past.
One more good-bye, perhaps the last
To Leudemanns-on-the-River.

LITTLE BLUE HOOD
Every morning and every night

There passes our window near the street,
A little girl with an eye so bright,
And a cheek so round and a lip so sweet!
The daintiest, jauntiest little miss
That ever any one longed to kiss,

She is neat as wax, and fresh to view,
And her look is wholesome, and clean, and good.
Whatever her gown, her hood is blue,
And so we call her our "Little Blue Hood,"
For we know not the name of the dear little lass,
But we call to each other to see her pass,

"Little Blue Hood is coming now!"
And we watch from the window while she goes by,
She has such a bonny, smooth, white brow,
And a fearless look in her long-lashed eye!
And a certain dignity wedded to grace
Seems to envelop her form and face.

Every morning, in sun or rain,
She walks by the window with sweet, grave air,
And never guesses behind the pane
We two are watching and thinking her fair;
Lovingly watching her down the street,
Dear little Blue Hood, bright and sweet.

Somebody ties that hood of blue
Under the face so fair to see,
Somebody loves her, beside we two,
Somebody kisses her, why can't we?
Dear Little Blue Hood fresh and fair,
Are you glad we love you, or don't you care?

NO SPRING
Up from the South come the birds that were banished,
Frightened away by the presence of frost.
Back to the vale comes the verdure that vanished,
Back to the forest the leaves that were lost.
Over the hillside the carpet of splendour,
Folded through Winter, Spring spreads down again;
Along the horizon, the tints that were tender,
Lost hues of Summer-time, burn bright as then.

Only the mountains' high summits are hoary,
To the ice-fettered river the sun gives a key.

Once more the gleaming shore lists to the story
Told by an amorous Summer-kissed sea.
All things revive that in Winter time perished,
The rose buds again in the light o' the sun,
All that was beautiful, all that was cherished,
Sweet things and dear things and all things save one.

Late, when the year and the roses were lying
Low with the ruins of Summer and bloom,
Down in the dust fell a love that was dying,
And the snow piled over it, and made it a tomb.
Lo! now the roses are budded for blossom
Lo! now the Summer is risen again.
Why dost thou bud not, O Love of my bosom?
Why dost thou rise not, and thrill me as then?

Life without love is a year without Summer,
Heart without love is a wood without song.
Rise then, revive then, thou indolent comer:
Why dost thou lie in the dark earth so long?
Rise! ah, thou can'st not! the rose-tree that sheddest
Its beautiful leaves, in the Springtime may bloom,
But of cold things the coldest, of dead things the deadest,
Love buried once, rises not from the tomb.
Green things may grow on the hillside and heather,
Birds seek the forest and build there and sing.
All things revive in the beautiful weather,
But unto a dead love there cometh no Spring.

MIDSUMMER

After the May time, and after the June time,
Rare with blossoms and perfumes sweet,
Cometh the round world's royal noon time,
The red midsummer of blazing heat.
When the sun, like an eye that never closes,
Bends on the earth its fervid gaze,
And the winds are still, and the crimson roses
Droop and wither and die in its rays.

Unto my heart has come that season,
O my lady, my worshipped one,
When over the stars of Pride and Reason
Sails Love's cloudless, noonday sun.
Like a great red ball in my bosom burning
With fires that nothing can quench or tame.
It glows till my heart itself seems turning

Into a liquid lake of flame.

The hopes half shy, and the sighs all tender,
The dreams and fears of an earlier day,
Under the noontide's royal splendour,
Droop like roses and wither away.
From the hills of doubt no winds are blowing,
From the isle of pain no breeze is sent.
Only the sun in a white heat glowing
Over an ocean of great content.

Sink, O my soul, in this golden glory,
Die, O my heart, in thy rapture-swoon,
For the Autumn must come with its mournful story,
And Love's midsummer will fade too soon.

A REMINISCENCE
I saw the wild honey-bee kissing a rose
A wee one, that grows
Down low on the bush, where her sisters above
Cannot see all that's done
As the moments roll on.
Nor hear all the whispers and murmurs of love.

They flaunt out their beautiful leaves in the sun,
And they flirt, every one,
With the wild bees who pass, and the gay butterflies.
And that wee thing in pink
Why, they never once think
That she's won a lover right under their eyes.

It reminded me, Kate, of a time, you know when!
You were so petite then,
Your dresses were short, and your feet were so small.
Your sisters, Maud-Belle
And Madeline, well,
They BOTH set their caps for me, after that ball.

How the blue eyes and black eyes smiled up in my face!
'Twas a neck-and-neck race,
Till that day when you opened the door in the hall,
And looked up and looked down,
With your sweet eyes of brown,
And YOU seemed so tiny, and I felt so tall.

Your sisters had sent you to keep me, my dear,

Till they should appear.
Then you were dismissed like a child in disgrace.
How meekly you went!
But your brown eyes, they sent
A thrill to my heart, and a flush to my face.

We always were meeting some way after that.
You hung up my hat,
And got it again, when I finished my call.
Sixteen, and SO sweet!
Oh, those cute little feet!
Shall I ever forget how they tripped down the hall?

Shall I ever forget the first kiss by the door,
Or the vows murmured o'er,
Or the rage and surprise of Maud-Belle? Well-a-day,
How swiftly time flows,
And who would suppose
That a BEE could have carried me so far away.

A GIRL'S FAITH
Across the miles that stretch between,
Through days of gloom or glad sunlight,
There shines a face I have not seen
Which yet doth make my world more bright.

He may be near, he may be far,
Or near or far I cannot see,
But faithful as the morning star
He yet shall rise and come to me.

What though fate leads us separate ways,
The world is round, and time is fleet.
A journey of a few brief days,
And face to face we two shall meet.

Shall meet beneath God's arching skies,
While suns shall blaze, or stars shall gleam,
And looking in each other's eyes
Shall hold the past but as a dream.

But round and perfect and complete,
Life like a star shall climb the height,
As we two press with willing feet
Together toward the Infinite.

And still behind the space between,
As back of dawns the sunbeams play,
There shines the face I have not seen,
Whose smile shall wake my world to-day.

TWO

One leaned on velvet cushions like a queen
To see him pass, the hero of an hour,
Whom men called great. She bowed with languid mien,
And smiled, and blushed, and knew her beauty's power.

One trailed her tinselled garments through the street,
And thrust aside the crowd, and found a place
So near, the blooded courser's prancing feet
Cast sparks of fire upon her painted face.

One took the hot-house blossoms from her breast,
And tossed them down, as he went riding by,
And blushed rose-red to see them fondly pressed
To bearded lips, while eye spoke unto eye.

One, bold and hardened with her sinful life,
Yet shrank and shivered painfully, because
His cruel glance cut keener than a knife,
The glance of him who made her what she was.

One was observed, and lifted up to fame,
Because the hero smiled upon her! while
One who was shunned and hated, found her shame
In basking in the death-light of his smile.

SLIPPING AWAY

Slipping away, slipping away!
Out of our brief year slips the May;
And Winter lingers, and Summer flies;
And Sorrow abideth, and Pleasure dies;
And the days are short, and the nights are long;
And little is right, and much is wrong.

Slipping away is the Summer time;
It has lost its rhythm and lilting rhyme
For the grace goes out of the day so soon,
And the tired headaches in the glare of noon,
And the way seems long to the hills that lie
Under the calm of the western sky.

Slipping away are the friends whose worth
Lent a glow to the sad old earth:
One by one they slip from our sight;
One by one their graves gleam white;
Or we count them lost by the crueller death
Of a trust betrayed, or a murdered faith.

Slipping away are the hopes that made
Bliss out of sorrow, and sun out of shade,
Slipping away is our hold on life;
And out of the struggle and wearing strife,
From joys that diminish, and woes that increase,
We are slipping away to the shores of Peace.

IS IT DONE?

It is done! in the fire's fitful flashes,
The last line has withered and curled.
In a tiny white heap of dead ashes
Lie buried the hopes of your world.
There were mad foolish vows in each letter,
It is well they have shrivelled and burned,
And the ring! oh, the ring was a fetter,
It was better removed and returned.

But ah, is it done? In the embers
Where letters and tokens were cast,
Have you burned up the heart that remembers,
And treasures its beautiful past?
Do you think in this swift reckless fashion
To ruthlessly burn and destroy
The months that were freighted with passion,
The dreams that were drunken with joy?

Can you burn up the rapture of kisses
That flashed from the lips to the soul,
Or the heart that grows sick for lost blisses
In spite of its strength of control?
Have you burned up the touch of warm fingers
That thrilled through each pulse and each vein,
Or the sound of a voice that still lingers
And hurts with a haunting refrain?

Is it done? is the life drama ended?
You have put all the lights out, and yet,
Though the curtain, rung down, has descended,

Can the actors go home and forget?
Ah, no! they will turn in their sleeping
With a strange restless pain in their hearts,
And in darkness, and anguish, and weeping,
Will dream they are playing their parts.

A LEAF

Somebody said, in the crowd, last eve,
That you were married, or soon to be.
I have not thought of you, I believe,
Since last we parted. Let me see:
Five long Summers have passed since then
Each has been pleasant in its own way
And you are but one of a dozen men
Who have played the suitor a Summer day.

But, nevertheless, when I heard your name,
Coupled with some one's, not my own,
There burned in my bosom a sudden flame,
That carried me back to the day that is flown.
I was sitting again by the laughing brook,
With you at my feet, and the sky above,
And my heart was fluttering under your look
The unmistakable look of Love.

Again your breath, like a South wind, fanned
My cheek, where the blushes came and went;
And the tender clasp of your strong, warm hand
Sudden thrills through my pulses sent.
Again you were mine by Love's own right
Mine for ever by Love's decree:
So for a moment it seemed last night,
When somebody mentioned your name to me.

Just for the moment I thought you mine
Loving me, wooing me, as of old.
The tale remembered seemed half divine
Though I held it lightly enough when told.
The past seemed fairer than when it was near,
As "blessings brighten when taking flight;"
And just for the moment I held you dear
When somebody mentioned your name last night.

AESTHETIC

In a garb that was guiltless of colours

She stood, with a dull, listless air
A creature of dumps and of dolours,
But most undeniably fair.

The folds of her garment fell round her,
Revealing the curve of each limb;
Well proportioned and graceful I found her,
Although quite alarmingly slim.

From the hem of her robe peeped one sandal
"High art" was she down to her feet;
And though I could not understand all
She said, I could see she was sweet.

Impressed by her limpness and languor,
I proffered a chair near at hand;
She looked back a mild sort of anger
Posed anew, and continued to stand.

Some praises I next tried to mutter
Of the fan that she held to her face;
She said it was "utterly utter,"
And waved it with languishing grace.

I then, in a strain quite poetic,
Begged her gaze on the bow in the sky,
She looked, said its curve was "aesthetic."
But the "tone was too dreadfully high."

Her lovely face, lit by the splendour
That glorified landscape and sea,
Woke thoughts that were daring and tender:
Did HER thoughts, too, rest upon me?

"Oh, tell me," I cried, growing bolder,
"Have I in your musings a place?"
"Well, yes," she said over her shoulder:
"I was thinking of nothing in space."

POEMS OF THE WEEK

SUNDAY
Lie still and rest, in that serene repose
That on this holy morning comes to those
Who have been burdened with the cares which make
The sad heart weary and the tired head ache.

Lie still and rest -
God's day of all is best.

MONDAY
Awake! arise! Cast off thy drowsy dreams!
Red in the East, behold the Morning gleams.
"As Monday goes, so goes the week," dames say.
Refreshed, renewed, use well the initial day.
And see! thy neighbour
Already seeks his labour.

TUESDAY
Another morning's banners are unfurled
Another day looks smiling on the world.
It holds new laurels for thy soul to win;
Mar not its grace by slothfulness or sin,
Nor sad, away,
Send it to yesterday.

WEDNESDAY
Half-way unto the end, the week's high noon.
The morning hours do speed away so soon!
And, when the noon is reached, however bright,
Instinctively we look toward the night.
The glow is lost
Once the meridian cross'd.

THURSDAY
So well the week has sped, hast thou a friend,
Go spend an hour in converse. It will lend
New beauty to thy labours and thy life
To pause a little sometimes in the strife.
Toil soon seems rude
That has no interlude.

FRIDAY
From feasts abstain; be temperate, and pray;
Fast if thou wilt; and yet, throughout the day,
Neglect no labour and no duty shirk:
Not many hours are left thee for thy work
And it were meet
That all should be complete.

SATURDAY
Now with the almost finished task make haste.
So near the night thou hast no time to waste.
Post up accounts, and let thy Soul's eyes look

For flaws and errors in Life's ledger-book.
When labours cease,
How sweet the sense of peace!

GHOSTS
There are ghosts in the room.
As I sit here alone, from the dark corners there
They come out of the gloom,
And they stand at my side and they lean on my chair.

There's the ghost of a Hope
That lighted my days with a fanciful glow.
In her hand is the rope
That strangled her life out. Hope was slain long ago.

But her ghost comes to-night,
With its skeleton face and expressionless eyes,
And it stands in the light,
And mocks me, and jeers me with sobs and with sighs.

There's the ghost of a Joy,
A frail, fragile thing, and I prized it too much,
And the hands that destroy
Clasped it close, and it died at the withering touch.

There's the ghost of a Love,
Born with joy, reared with hope, died in pain and unrest,
But he towers above
All the others, this ghost: yet a ghost at the best.

I am weary, and fain
Would forget all these dead: but the gibbering host
Make my struggle in vain,
In each shadowy corner there lurketh a ghost.

FLEEING AWAY
My thoughts soar not as they ought to soar,
Higher and higher on soul-lent wings;
But ever and often, and more and more
They are dragged down earthward by little things,
By little troubles and little needs,
As a lark might be tangled among the weeds.

My purpose is not what it ought to be,
Steady and fixed, like a star on high,

But more like a fisherman's light at sea;
Hither and thither it seems to fly
Sometimes feeble, and sometimes bright,
Then suddenly lost in the gloom of night.

My life is far from my dream of life
Calmly contented, serenely glad;
But, vexed and worried by daily strife,
It is always troubled, and oft times sad
And the heights I had thought I should reach one day
Grow dimmer and dimmer, and farther away.

My heart finds never the longed-for rest;
Its worldly striving, its greed for gold,
Chilled and frightened the calm-eyed guest,
Who sometimes sought me in days of old;
And ever fleeing away from me
Is the higher self that I long to be.

ALL MAD
"He is mad as a hare, poor fellow,
And should be in chains," you say.
I haven't a doubt of your statement,
But who isn't mad, I pray?
Why, the world is a great asylum,
And people are all insane,
Gone daft with pleasure or folly,
Or crazed with passion and pain.

The infant who shrieks at a shadow,
The child with his Santa Claus faith,
The woman who worships Dame Fashion,
Each man with his notions of death,
The miser who hoards up his earnings,
The spendthrift who wastes them too soon,
The scholar grown blind in his delving,
The lover who stares at the moon.

The poet who thinks life a paean,
The cynic who thinks it a fraud,
The youth who goes seeking for pleasure,
The preacher who dares talk of God,
All priests with their creeds and their croaking,
All doubters who dare to deny,
The gay who find aught to wake laughter,
The sad who find aught worth a sigh,

Whoever is downcast or solemn,
Whoever is gleeful and glad,
Are only the dupes of delusions
We are all of us, all of us mad.

HIDDEN GEMS

We know not what lies in us, till we seek;
Men dive for pearls, they are not found on shore,
The hillsides most unpromising and bleak
Do sometimes hide the ore.

Go, dive in the vast ocean of thy mind,
O man! far down below the noisy waves,
Down in the depths and silence thou mayst find
Rare pearls and coral caves.

Sink thou a shaft into the mine of thought;
Be patient, like the seekers after gold;
Under the rocks and rubbish lieth what
May bring thee wealth untold.

Reflected from the vastly Infinite,
However dulled by earth, each human mind
Holds somewhere gems of beauty and of light
Which, seeking, thou shalt find.

BY-AND-BYE

"By-and-bye," the maiden sighed "by-and-bye
He will claim me for his bride,
Hope is strong and time is fleet;
Youth is fair, and love is sweet,
Clouds will pass that fleck my sky,
He will come back by-and-bye, by-and-bye."

"By-and-bye," the soldier said, "by-and-bye,
After I have fought and bled,
I shall go home from the wars,
Crowned with glory, seamed with scars.
Joy will flash from some one's eye
When she greets me by-and-bye, by-and-bye."

"By-and-bye," the mother cried, "by-and-bye,
Strong and sturdy at my side,
Like a staff supporting me,
Will my bonnie baby be.

Break my rest, then, wail and cry
Thou'lt repay me by-and-bye, by-and-bye."

Fleeting years of time have sped, hurried by
Still the maiden is unwed:
All unknown the soldier lies,
Buried under alien skies;
And the son, with blood-shot eye,
Saw his mother starve and die.
God in Heaven! dost Thou on high,
Keep the promised "by-and-bye", by-and-bye?

OVER THE MAY HILL
All through the night time, and all through the day time,
Dreading the morning and dreading the night,
Nearer and nearer we drift to the May time
Season of beauty and season of blight,
Leaves on the linden, and sun on the meadow,
Green in the garden, and bloom everywhere,
Gloom in my heart, and a terrible shadow,
Walks by me, sits by me, stands by my chair.

Oh, but the birds by the brooklet are cheery,
Oh, but the woods show such delicate greens,
Strange how you droop and how soon you are weary
Too well I know what that weariness means.
But how could I know in the crisp winter weather
(Though sometimes I noticed a catch in your breath),
Riding and singing and dancing together,
How could I know you were racing with death?

How could I know when we danced until morning,
And you were the gayest of all the gay crowd
With only that shortness of breath for a warning,
How could I know that you danced for a shroud?
Whirling and whirling through moonlight and starlight.
Rocking as lightly as boats on the wave,
Down in your eyes shone a deep light, a far light,
How could I know 'twas the light to your grave?

Day by day, day by day, nearing and nearing,
Hid under greenness, and beauty and bloom,
Cometh the shape and the shadow I'm fearing,
"Over the May hill" is waiting your tomb.
The season of mirth and of music is over
I have danced my last dance, I have sung my last song,

Under the violets, under the clover,
My heart and my love will be lying ere long

FOES

Thank Fate for foes! I hold mine dear
As valued friends. He cannot know
The zest of life who runneth here
His earthly race without a foe.

I saw a prize. "Run," cried my friend;
"'Tis thine to claim without a doubt."
But ere I half-way reached the end,
I felt my strength was giving out.

My foe looked on the while I ran;
A scornful triumph lit his eyes.
With that perverseness born in man,
I nerved myself, and won the prize.

All blinded by the crimson glow
Of sin's disguise, I tempted Fate.
"I knew thy weakness!" sneered my foe,
I saved myself, and balked his hate.

For half my blessings, half my gain,
I needs must thank my trusty foe;
Despite his envy and disdain,
He serves me well where'er I go.

So may I keep him to the end,
Nor may his enmity abate:
More faithful than the fondest friend,
He guards me ever with his hate.

FRIENDSHIP

Dear friend, I pray thee, if thou wouldst be proving
Thy strong regard for me,
Make me no vows. Lip-service is not loving;
Let thy faith speak for thee.

Swear not to me that nothing can divide us
So little such oaths mean.
But when distrust and envy creep beside us
Let them not come between.

Say not to me the depths of thy devotion
Are deeper than the sea;
But watch, lest doubt or some unkind emotion
Embitter them for me.

Vow not to love me ever and forever,
Words are such idle things;
But when we differ in opinions, never
Hurt me by little stings.

I'm sick of words: they are so lightly spoken,
And spoken, are but air.
I'd rather feel thy trust in me unbroken
Than list thy words so fair.

If all the little proofs of trust are heeded,
If thou art always kind,
No sacrifice, no promise will be needed
To satisfy my mind.

TWO SAT DOWN

Two sat down in the morning time,
One to sing and one to spin.
All men listened the song sublime
But no one listened the dull wheel's din.

The singer sat in a pleasant nook,
And sang of a life that was fair and sweet,
While the spinner sat with a steadfast look,
Busily plying her hands and feet.

The singer sang on with a rose in her hair,
And all men listened her dulcet tone;
And the spinner spun on with a dull despair
Down in her heart as she sat alone.

But lo! on the morrow no one said
Aught of the singer or what she sang.
Men were saying: "Behold this thread,"
And loud the praise of the spinner rang.

The world has forgotten the singer's name
Her rose is faded, her songs are old;
But far o'er the ocean the spinner's fame
Yet is blazoned in lines of gold.

BOUND AND FREE

Come to me, Love! Come on the wings of the wind!
Fly as the ring-dove would fly to his mate!
Leave all your cares and your sorrows behind!
Leave all the fears of your future to Fate!
Come! and our skies shall be glad with the gold
That paled into gray when you parted from me.
Come! but remember that, just as of old,
You must be bound, Love, and I must be free.

Life has lost savour since you and I parted;
I have been lonely, and you have been sad.
Youth is too brief to be sorrowful-hearted
Come! and again let us laugh and be glad.
Lips should not sigh that are fashioned to kiss
Breasts should not ache that joy's secrets have found.
Come! but remember, in spite of all this,
I must be free, Love, while you must be bound.

You must be bound to be true while you live,
And I keep my freedom for ever, as now.
You must ask only for that which I give
Kisses and love-words, but never a vow.
Come! I am lonely, and long for your smile,
Bring back the lost lovely Summer to me!
Come! but remember, remember the while,
That you must be bound, Love, and I must be free.

AQUILEIA

[On the election of the Roman Emperor Maximus, by the Senate, A.D.
238, a powerful army, headed by the Thracian giant Maximus, laid siege
to Aquileia. Though poorly prepared for war, the constancy of her citizens
rendered her impregnable. The women of Aquileia cut off their hair to
make ropes for the military engines. The small body of troops was
directed by Chrispinus, a Lieutenant of the Senate. Apollo was the deity
supposed to protect them. Gibbon's Roman History.]

"The ropes, the ropes! Apollo send us ropes,"
Chrispinus cried, "or death attends our hopes."
Then panic reigned, and many a mournful sound
Hurt the cleft air; for where could ropes be found?

Up rose a Roman mother; tall was she
As her own son, a youth of noble height.
A little child was clinging to her knee -

She loosed his twining arms and put him down,
And her dark eyes flashed with a sudden light.

How like a queen she stood! her royal crown,
The rich dark masses of her splendid hair.
Just flecked with spots of sunshine here and there,
Twined round her brow; 'twas like a coronet,
Where gems of gold lie bedded deep in jet.

She loosed the comb that held the shining strands,
And threaded out the meshes with her hands.
The purple mass fell to her garment's hem.
A queen new clothed without her diadem
She stood before her subjects.

"Now," she cried,
"Give me thy sword, Julianus!" And her son
Unsheathed the blade (that had not left his side
Save when it sought a foeman's blood to shed),
Awed by her regal bearing, and obeyed.

With the white beauty of her firm fair hand
She clasped the hilt; then severed, one by one,
Her gold-flecked purple tresses. Strand on strand,
Free e'en as foes had fallen by that blade,
Robbed of its massive wealth of curl and coil,
Yet like some antique model, rose her head
In all its classic beauty.

"See!" she said,
And pointed to the shining mound of hair;
"Apollo makes swift answer to thy prayer,
Chrispinus. Quick! now, soldiers, to thy toil!"
Forth from a thousand throats what seemed one voice
Rose shrilly, filling all the air with cheer.

"Lo!" quoth the foe, "our enemies rejoice!"
Well might the Thracian giant quake with fear!
For while skilled hands caught up the gleaming threads
And bound them into cords, a hundred heads
Yielded their beauteous tresses to the sword,
And cast them down to swell the precious hoard.

Nor was the noble sacrifice in vain
Another day beheld the giant slain.

WISHES FOR A LITTLE GIRL

What would I ask the kindly fates to give
To crown her life, if I could have my way?
My strongest wishes would be negative,
If they would but obey.

Give her not greatness. For great souls must stand
Alone and lonely in this little world:
Cleft rocks that show the great Creator's hand,
Thither by earthquakes hurled.

Give her not genius. Spare her the cruel pain
Of finding her whole life a prey for daws;
Of hearing with quickened sense and burning brain
The world's sneer-tinged applause.

Give her not perfect beauty's gifts. For then
Her truthful mirror would infuse her mind
With love for self, and for the praise of men,
That lowers woman-kind.

But make her fair and comely to the sight,
Give her more heart than brain, more love than pride.
Let her be tender-thoughted, cheerful, bright,
Some strong man's star and guide.

Not vainly questioning why she was sent
Into this restless world of toil and strife,
Let her go bravely on her way, content
To make the best of life.

ROMNEY

Nay, Romney, nay, I will not hear you say
Those words again: "I love you, love you sweet!"
You are profane, blasphemous. I repeat,
You are no actor for so grand a play.

You love with all your heart? Well, that may be;
Some cups are fashioned shallow. Should I try
To quench my thirst from one of those, when dry
I who have had a full bowl proffered me

A new bowl brimming with a draught divine,
One single taste thrilled to the finger-tips?
Think you I even care to bathe my lips
With this poor sweetened water you call wine?

And though I spilled the nectar ere 'twas quaffed,
And broke the bowl in wanton folly, yet
I would die of my thirst ere I would wet
My burning lips with any meaner draught.

So leave me, Romney. One who has seen a play
Enacted by a star cannot endure
To see it rendered by an amateur.
You know not what Love is, ow go away!

MY HOME

This is the place that I love the best,
A little brown house like a ground-bird's nest,
Hid among grasses, and vines, and trees,
Summer retreat of the birds and bees.

The tenderest light that ever was seen
Sifts through the vine-made window screen
Sifts and quivers, and flits and falls
On home-made carpets and gray-hung walls.

All through June, the west wind free
The breath of the clover brings to me.
All through the languid July day
I catch the scent of the new-mown hay.

The morning glories and scarlet vine
Over the doorway twist and twine;
And every day, when the house is still,
The humming-bird comes to the window-sill.

In the cunningest chamber under the sun
I sink to sleep when the day is done;
And am waked at morn, in my snow-white bed,
By a singing-bird on the roof o'erhead.

Better than treasures brought from Rome
Are the living pictures I see at home
My aged father, with frosted hair,
And mother's face like a painting rare
Far from the city's dust and heat,
I get but sounds and odours sweet.
Who can wonder I love to stay,
Week after week, here hidden away,
In this sly nook that I love the best -

The little brown house, like a ground-bird's nest?

TO MARRY OR NOT TO MARRY? A GIRL'S REVERIE
Mother says, "Be in no hurry,
Marriage oft means care and worry."

Auntie says, with manner grave,
"Wife is synonym for slave."

Father asks, in tones commanding,
"How does Bradstreet rate his standing?"

Sister crooning to her twins,
Sighs, "With marriage care begins."

Grandma, near life's closing days,
Murmurs, "Sweet are girlhood's ways."

Maud, twice widowed ("sod and grass")
Looks at me and moans "Alas!"

They are six, and I am one,
Life for me has just begun.

They are older, calmer, wiser:
Age should aye be youth's adviser.

They must know, and yet, dear me,
When in Harry's eyes I see

All the world of love there burning
On my six advisers turning,

I make answer, "Oh, but Harry
Is not like most men who marry.

"Fate has offered me a prize,
Life with love means Paradise.

"Life without it is not worth
All the foolish joys of earth."

So, in spite of all they say,
I shall name the wedding day.

AN AFTERNOON

I am stirred by the dream of an afternoon
Of a perfect day, though it was not June;
The lilt of winds, and the droning tune
That a busy city was humming.

And a bronze-brown head, and lips like wine
Leaning out through the window-vine
A-list for steps that were maybe mine
Eager steps that were coming.

I can see it all, as a dreamer may
The tender smile on your lips that day,
And the glow on your cheek as we rode away
Into the golden weather.

And a love-light shone in your eyes of brown
I swear there did! as we drove down
The crowded avenue out of the town,
Through shadowy lanes, together:

Drove out into the sunset-skies
That glowed with wonderful crimson dyes;
And with soul and spirit, and heart and eyes,
We silently drank their splendour.

But the golden glory that lit the place
Was not alone from the sunset's grace
For I saw in your fair, uplifted face
A light that was wondrously tender.

I say I saw it. And yet to-day
I ask myself, in a cynical way,
Was it only a part you had learned to play,
To see me act the lover?

And I curse myself for a fool. And yet
I would willingly die without one regret
Could I bring back the day whose sun has set
And you and live it over.

RIVER AND SEA

We stood by the river that swept
In its glory and grandeur away;
But never a pulse o' me leapt,
And you wondered at me that day.

We stood by the lake as it lay
With its dimpled face turned to the light;
Was it strange I had nothing to say
To so fair and enchanting a sight?

I look on your tresses of gold
You are fair and a thing to be loved
Do you think I am heartless and cold
That I look and am wholly unmoved?

One answer, dear friend, I will make
To the questions your eyes ask of me:
"Talk not of the river or lake
To those who have looked on the sea"

WHAT HAPPENS?

When thy hand touches mine, through all the mesh
Of intricate and interlaced veins
Shoot swift delights that border on keen pains:
Flesh thrills to thrilling flesh.

When in thine eager eyes I look to find
A comrade to my thought, thy ready brain
Delves down and makes its inmost meaning plain:
Mind answers unto mind.

When hands and eyes are hid by seas that roll
Wide wastes between us, still so near thou art
I count the very pulses of thy heart:
Soul speaketh unto soul.

So every law, or human or divine,
In heart and brain and spirit makes thee mine.

POSSESSION

That which we had we still possess,
Though leaves may drop and stars may fall;
No circumstance can make it less,
Or take it from us, all in all.

That which is lost we did not own;
We only held it for a day
A leaf by careless breezes blown;
No fate could take our own away.

I hold it as a changeless law
From which no soul can sway or swerve,
We have that in us which will draw
Whate'er we need or most deserve.

Even as the magnet to the steel
Our souls are to our best desires;
The Fates have hearts and they can feel
They know what each true life requires.

We think we lose when we most gain;
We call joys ended ere begun;
When stars fade out do skies complain,
Or glory in the rising sun?

No fate could rob us of our own
No circumstance can make it less;
What time removes was but a loan,
For what was ours we still possess.

Ella Wheeler Wilcox – A Short Biography

Ella Wheeler was born on 5th November, 1850, on a farm in the village of Johnstown, Rock County, Wisconsin. Her parents, Marcus H. Wheeler and Sarah Pratt Wheeler, already had three children. A year earlier the family had moved from Vermont after Marcus's attempts at show business failed and becoming a farmer was his response. With Ella's birth they moved again. This time further north to Madison.

Ella was a gifted child, writing poetry and novels from an early age. The family was poor but her parents believed in education, and whilst little could be afforded they helped as best they could most usefully with grammar, spelling and vocabulary. Her initial education was at the local district school in the village of Windsor, now re-named in her honour as Ella Wheeler Wilcox School.

During her thirteenth year subscriptions the family had been receiving from the New York Mercury, a popular periodical, ceased. This greatly upset her. Life on the farm was lonely and the magazine had been a source of comfort and information about the big world beyond the farm. The family could not afford its own subscription so Ella had to make other plans.

Her writing ambitions were central to this. She wrote two essays but now had to obtain stamps so she could get her submissions in front of editors. She was corresponding with a young girl, Jean, who was in the freshman class at Madison University. Assuring her friend of future payment she enclosed the letter and essays for the New York Mercury.

By 1866, Jean, at Ella's behest, sent a list of all the monthlies and weeklies on the newsstands and Ella was hard at work saving pennies for postage as she began to mail them en masse with her works. Quickly her family lent their support to help out with her endeavours. Ella's mother especially had always thought her daughter would be the one to find the fame, travel and recognition that she had wanted herself and seeing the efforts Ella was putting in she was only to glad to help.

Soon the house the house was filled with ALL the periodicals. Editors would send magazines, books, pictures, bric-a-brac and tableware in response to Ella's requests and works. Being able to earn these items brought her great satisfaction and honed her skills.

She remembers the period in her autobiography:

"The very first verses I sent for publication were unmercifully "guyed" by my beloved "Mercury." The editor urged me to keep to prose and to avoid any further attempts at rhyme. He said that, while this criticism would wound me temporarily, it would eventually confer a favour on me and the world at large.

"My first check came from Frank Leslie's publishing house. I wrote asking for one of his periodicals to be sent to me in return for three little poems I had composed in one day. In reply came a check for ten dollars, saying I must select which one of some thirteen publications they issued at that time.

This bit of crisp paper opened a perfect floodgate of aspiration, inspiration and ambition for me. I had not thought of earning money so soon. I had expected to obtain only books, magazines and articles of use and beauty from the editor's prize-lists; and I had not supposed verses to be saleable. I wrote them because they came to me, but I expected to be a novelist like Mrs. Southworth and May Agens Fleming in time - that was the goal of my dreams. The check from Leslie was a revelation. I walked, talked, thought and dreamed in verse after that. A day which passed without a poem from my pen I considered lost and misused. Two each day was my idea of industry, and I once achieved eight. They sold, the majority, for three dollars or five dollars each. Sometimes I got ten dollars for a poem, that was always an event. Short love-stories, over which I laboured painfully, as story writing was an acquired habit, also added to my income, bringing me ten or fifteen dollars, and once in a while larger sums, from "Peterson's," "Demorest's," "Harper's Bazaar" and the "Chimney Corner."

Ella was beginning to understand the route to success and had the work ethic and creativity to turn it to her advantage. Ella would write her daily quota of poems and other works and then send them out to editors in the hope of getting them published.

It was also about this time that she also left the Country school. Her record in grammar, spelling, reading had of course been excellent but she had a horror of mathematics preferring to spend as much time as possible in the world of her imagination. Ella's talent and determination was such that by now, after she graduated from High School she was already well known in her state as a young writer.

In this she was encouraged by her mother, who despised her own life and felt herself and her family superior to all her neighbours and was forever impressing on the young teenager that her life would blossom and she would achieve success as a writer.

In 1867 her parents sent her to Madison where she was a junior in the Female College, a part of the University of Wisconsin. Ella wanted to spend all of her time writing and begged to come home. She didn't feel the need for further education and was painfully aware of the difference between her homemade clothes and the dresses of city girl. These and other differences caused her to feel left out and not part of the group. After many requests her parents relented and she was allowed home to continue her writing.

In 1870 she was offered employment at $45 a month to edit the literary department of a publication by the magazine's Milwaukee Editor. She accepted, but the hours and work were not to her liking and after three months the magazine folded and her single experience of working in an office was over. Now she was to be a full time author.

In 1872 she published her first book. It was an unusual step as it was a book of poems entitled 'Drops Of Water: Poems' that were solely about abstinence. Published by the National Temperance society it reflected her views on the evils of alcohol and earned her a $50 fee.

She published further books over the next decade but it wasn't until 1883 and the rather racy, for those times, publication of Poems of Passion that her success moved suddenly forward. It was an immediate and large scale success selling over 60,000 in two years.

That same year was also noteworthy for she was engaged to be married. Robert Wilcox was one of many suitors to the young Ella. He was a silver salesman from Meriden, Connecticut. Although they only met three times before the wedding it was to be the relationship that defined her life and much of her work. They married the following year in 1884.

Her most famous poem, "Solitude", was first published on 25th February, 1883 in an issue of The New York Sun. The inspiration for the poem came as she was travelling to attend the State Governor's inaugural ball in Madison, Wisconsin. Whilst travelling to the celebration she was sitting next to a young woman, dressed in black, who was in obvious distress. Ella comforted her for the whole journey. Recalling the widow's emotional state Ella wrote:

Laugh, and the world laughs with you;
Weep, and you weep alone.
For the sad old earth must borrow its mirth
But has trouble enough of its own

She sent the poem to the Sun and received $5 for her effort. It was collected in the book Poems of Passion shortly after in May 1883.

The newlyweds lived for a short time in Robert's home town of Meriden, Connecticut, before moving to New York City and then to Granite Bay in the Short Beach area of Branford, Connecticut. They built two homes and several cottages on Long Island Sound where they would hold gatherings of their literary and artistic friends.

On May 27, 1887, Ella gave birth to a son. Tragically he was only to survive for a few short hours.

In the early years of their marriage, they both developed an interest in theosophy, New Thought, and spiritualism. As this developed Robert and Ella Wheeler Wilcox promised each other that whoever died first would return and attempt to communicate with the other.

Ella had by now published many books of poetry as well as novels and other writings. Her writing life was filled with success on a national scale. Some volumes were collections based on a theme others on a particular time. Some of her war poetry that centred on the Great War in Europe is quite compelling. As she was never considered literary but rather mass market a lot of her work has not received the recognition that other lesser writers have obtained.

In 1916 after thirty years of marriage Robert Wilcox died. Ella was naturally devastated and desperate. Rather than dissipate her grief seemed to grow ever more intense as the days and weeks went by with no message from him.   She journeyed to California to see the Rosicrucian astrologer, Max Heindel, seeking help in her sorrow as to why she had no word from Robert. She writes:

"In talking with Max Heindel, the leader of the Rosicrucian Philosophy in California, he made very clear to me the effect of intense grief. Mr. Heindel assured me that I would come in touch with the spirit of my husband when I learned to control my sorrow. I replied that it seemed strange to me that an omnipotent God could not send a flash of his light into a suffering soul to bring its conviction when most needed. Did you ever stand beside a clear pool of water, asked Mr. Heindel, and see the trees and skies repeated therein? And did you ever cast a stone into that pool and see it clouded and turmoiled, so it gave no reflection? Yet the skies and trees were waiting above to be reflected when the waters grew calm. So God and your husband's spirit wait to show themselves to you when the turbulence of sorrow is quieted".

It seemed good advice. She wrote herself a short affirmative prayer to help calm her inner turmoil and would repeat it to herself over and over:

"I am the living witness: The dead live: And they speak through us and to us: And I am the voice that gives this glorious truth to the suffering world: I am ready, God: I am ready, Christ: I am ready, Robert."

She had already written in 1915 a booklet 'What I Know About New Thought which had sold over 50,000 copies. These and other books on New Thought, together with her expanding efforts to educate a wider audience to the powers of positive thinking, were a great comfort to her.

Ella expresses this unique blend of New Thought, Spiritualism and Reincarnation with these powerful words:

"As we think, act, and live here today, we built the structures of our homes in spirit realms after we leave earth, and we build karma for future lives, thousands of years to come, on this earth or other planets. Life will assume new dignity, and labour new interest for us, when we come to the knowledge that death is but a continuation of life and labour, in higher planes".

Ella fell ill in France in early 1919. It was breast cancer. She was taken initially to England and then back to her home. She died of the cancer on October 31, 1919.

Her final words in her autobiography 'The Worlds and I' were:

"From this mighty storehouse (of God, and the hierarchies of Spiritual Beings) we may gather wisdom and knowledge, and receive light and power, as we pass through this preparatory room of earth, which is only one of the innumerable mansions in our Father's house. Think on these things".

A Concise Bibliography

1872 Drops of water, poems.
1873 Shells.
1876 Maurine.
1883 Poems of Passion.
1886 Mal Moule'e, a novel.
1886 Perdita, and other stories.
1888 The Adventures of Miss Volney.
1888 Poems of Pleasure.
1891 A Double Life.
1891 How Salvator Won, and other recitations.
1892 Was it Suicide?
1892 The Beautiful Land of Nod.
1892 An Erring Woman's Love.
1892 Sweet Danger.
1893 The Song of the Sandwich.
1893 Men, Women and Emotions.
1896 An Ambitious Man.
1896 Custer, and other poems.
1897 Three Women.
1897 Roger Merritt's Crime.
1901 Every-day Thoughts in Prose and Verse.
1901 Poems of Power.
1902 The Heart of the New Thought.
1902 Kingdom of Love and How Salvator Won.
1902 The Other Woman's Husband.
1902 Poems of Life.
1904 Around the Year with Ella Wheeler Wilcox.
1904 A Woman of the World.
1905 Mizpah; or, the story of Esther, poetical drama in four acts.
1905 Poems of Love.
1905 Poems of Reflection.
1905 The Story of a literary career.
1906 Poems of Sentiment.
1906 New Thought pastels.
1906 Poems of Peace.
1907 The Kingdom of love, and other poems.
1907 The Love Sonnets of Abelard and Heloise.
1908 New Thought - common sense and what life means to me.

1908   Poems of Cheer.
1908   Selected Poems.
1909   Poems of Progress and New Thought Pastels.
1909   Sailing Sunny Seas.
1910   Diary of a Faithless Husband.
1910   The New Hawaiian Girl; a play.
1910   Poems of Experience.
1910   Yesterdays.
1911   Are you Alive?
1912   Picked Poems.
1912   Gems from Ella Wheeler Wilcox.
1912   The Englishman and other Poems.
1914   Poems of Problems.
1914   The art of Being Alive.
1914   Cameos.
1914   Lest we Forget.
1914   Poems of Ella Wheeler Wilcox.
1915   Poems of Optimism.
1916   World Voices.
1916   More Poems.
1916   Poems of Purpose.
1917   Poetical Works of Ella Wheeler Wilcox.
1918   Sonnets of Sorrow and Triumph.
1918   The Worlds and I.
1919   Poems.
1919   Cinema Poems and others.
1919   Hello Boys!

Published Posthumously
1920   Poems of Affection.
1920   Great Thoughts For Each Day's Life.
1924   Collected Poems of Ella Wheeler Wilcox.
1927   Gems from E.W.Wilcox

Made in the USA
Middletown, DE
01 October 2020

20948889R00042